My First

Step-by-Step Puppy Tra

Gregory Davis

Gregory Davis

CONTENTS

1. A New Puppy: Day One **(1)**

2. Leashes and Leash Training **(19)**

3. How to Hold/Handle Your Puppy **(25)**

4. Puppy Feeding 101: Food & Nutrition **(31)**

5. Housetraining/Housebreaking Your Puppy **(37)**

6. Crate Training Your Puppy **(51)**

7. Puppy Emotions and Mental Well-Being **(57)**

8. All About Obedience **(75)**

9. Puppy Training FAQs **(101)**

10. Conclusion **(113)**

My First Puppy

1

A New Puppy: Day One

Allow me to start off by welcoming you to 'My First Puppy' - the only puppy training guide for beginners which takes you through all the essentials of owning, caring for and training your new fluffy little one. This guidebook has been designed to make everything as easy and straight-forward as possible so that there is no confusion and getting your puppy off to the best possible start is a breeze.

Not many guidebooks provide a comprehensive program for first-time puppy owners, and that's where we come in! Even if you know next to nothing about puppies, this guide has you covered. I have minimized the use of complicated terminology and where it does exist, a definition and clear elaboration is sure to follow.

The main aim of this book is to give you a detailed yet easy-to-follow scope of how to properly train your puppy so that they can develop into the best possible adult dogs. Puppies are just like us in that they require special care, have individual needs, complicated psyches and more than anything, lots and lots of love to give. Regardless of anything that you might have read about the difficulty of puppy training, what is certain is that dogs, whether you adopt them as little pups or get them when they're a lot older, truly are the best companions that a person could have and they can change your life for the better. It isn't an exaggeration when dog owners claim that their fluffy friends are integral parts of the family unit and you will find that out for yourself very quickly.

How To Use This Guide

This unique and comprehensive guide has two purposes: to help you get started with basic puppy training and to give you a detailed insight into the common behavioral and physical problems your puppy might face in the initial weeks and months of looking after him/her. What's more is that this book lays out in a straight forward manner the essential aspects of puppy care and training. Hopefully, you will find this handbook to be an invaluable resource as you experience the most rewarding time as a dog owner - the successful transition of your little fluffy family member from puppyhood into adulthood. Owning a puppy, especially without prior experience, can seem like a daunting prospect and there is a lot of responsibility that comes with it. However, it is my hope that you will find that this book cuts out a lot of the stress and uncertainty that you might face when confronting the changes that your puppy will undoubtedly go through. In spite of the stress of owning a puppy, you must enjoy the experience as much as possible and love your young fluffy friend with all of your heart.

Unlike other guidebooks, this one is a sort of step-by-step program for first-time puppy owners that takes you through the various stages after bringing your puppy home for the very first time. Even if you know practically nothing about puppies, this guide ought to provide you with a solid basis of understanding for puppy care. Wherever possible, complicated and ambiguous language, such as expert terminology, has been explained in an easy-to-follow manner.

With concerns to puppy related issues, it's vital to remember that puppies depend heavily on their owner(s) i.e. you! Every action you do in caring for them will impact how they experience you, others and the world around them. They have been taken away from their mothers and siblings where they would have learned how to behave in a very different context. That's why it's key that training your puppy is done correctly, and no shortcuts are taken under any circumstance. Because of this reason, among numerous others, it is completely worth putting in the effort, time and patience needed to raise and train a puppy.

I will clarify from the get-go that I'm not just an author. I'm a long-term dog owner and have had dogs for over two decades. As well as having worked with them, I've volunteered for shelters, been a behavior consultant and more personally, I've owned and raised puppies of multiple breeds. So I do speak from experience and as such, I certainly know how difficult it is to raise a puppy - especially if you're inexperienced and/or are a first-time dog owner. Do not worry though! This book cuts out all the fluff (no pun intended!) and gets right to the important information for raising a puppy. In this guide, every focal aspect of puppy raising and training will be covered. I am also aware that every dog is unique with their own personality and behavior. However, the steps you will find in these pages will be invaluable no matter what breed your puppy is.

This first chapter will provide an outline for what to expect on day one - when your puppy comes home for the first time. I understand completely that the first day is an intimidating time. You have a lot of questions and things to consider. On top of racing thoughts and anxieties regarding whether or not you have everything your puppy will need (crates, toys and so on), you have training and initial care to worry about. For many first time owners, knowing where to begin with puppy training can seem like a hard prospect, but take a deep breath!

You must take things one step at a time.

The start of your journey with your fluffy new friend is a pivotal time. From the very beginning, it is indispensable that you display a responsible attitude as well as a cocktail of patience and rationale. I cannot overstate how essential these traits are on your behalf. It's also very important to bear in mind that your puppy is most likely extremely nervous and confused too - so you aren't the only one(s)! Providing your puppy with a stable environment within the first days and weeks after bringing him/her home cannot be overstated.

Canines are extremely perceptive and they develop impressions about their surroundings very quickly. Whether it's a dog or a wolf, canines in the wild must adapt to their environment fast for survival and to find belonging within their pack. This is an advantage to owning a puppy because puppies are young and impressionable. If you take the right steps to encourage them to be independent, curious, social and disciplined (they are outlined throughout this book), they will be well-behaved and make for ideal and loving companions - which is ultimately what you want!

From day one, it's evident that enthusiasm and excitement are going to be present for all owners. The novelty mixed with anticipation of having a puppy is a combination we all experience. This is fantastic don't get me wrong, and I would never want to discourage anyone from being ecstatic to be bringing home their new adorable bundle of fluff.

BUT at the same time, this excitement can lead to an unhealthy start if you are not careful. It isn't uncommon to find puppy owners and families wanting to play with the puppy, feed him/her, cuddle them and be overbearing in a short and intense period of time. While this emotional attachment might seem like a positive thing, you should try your best as an individual/couple/family to remember that puppies are easily overwhelmed, especially at a young age, and this level of emotional nirvana isn't the best for your puppy. Of course, as time goes on and your puppy grows up, you might find that your puppy loves to receive huge amounts of affection and love. Every dog is different but when you get your puppy for the first time, assume that they're in a vulnerable state and are quite uncertain as to where they are. Be gentle with them and have lots of patience with them. Puppies need to take their time to make sense of their new home - it's a novel world for them to adjust to. Many new smells, faces and so on.

What You Can Do as a Responsible Owner?

All owners should **want** to be responsible. Just like when you have a new baby, there's a lot to get used to and often a big checklist of things to do and to sort out. When starting out, with concern to puppies, something vital to always keep at the forefront of your mind is the question 'what is my puppy feeling/thinking'? While this sounds like a silly question, it isn't. As humans, we anthropomorphize emotions of other animals and project our own feelings onto them. Being a responsible owner means trying to think like your puppy to ensure he/she is comfortable. I've seen so many occasions of owners smothering their puppy and claiming that their new little fluffy friend 'must be' happy because they are. The truth of the matter is - you don't know and the best thing to do is comprehend puppy behavior in regards to how they relate to their surroundings.

Of all the elements of puppy emotions when they join a new home, the important thing to note about them is that just like other infant canines, puppies work out hierarchy very quickly. Establishing order is something they are experts at. If you let your puppy sleep on your bed the first night and don't put in place set-in-stone rules, this will work against you very quickly. In fact, studies have time and time again shown that puppies who were trained from the very first day comprehend obedience three times better than puppies who weren't trained until the second month of being in a new household.

What's more is that if you don't establish your rules and are lazy with regards to your approach to puppy training, when the novelty of owning a new puppy wears off, your new dog will end up breaking the rules and you'll be the one struggling to clean up after him/her.

By all means be happy and show excitement but remember that the reason you got a puppy in first place was to love and protect them. Much like a human child, this responsibility comes will rules, boundaries and ensuring your puppy doesn't take over and exhibit bad behavior which becomes even more of a problem as he/she gets older.

Why do I say this? Because dogs are pack animals. Humans and intelligent hominids function differently. While we're both social creatures, dogs have an inherent sort of hierarchy. They mentally try to establish a sense of who is on top and leader. Since there are (usually) no other dogs around, or not many of them if you **do** have other animals, a lack of training from the first few days will mean that they can do what they want and that they have authority over you and the rest of the family.

Another reason why discipline from day one is so crucial is that when puppies are separated from their mother, their psyches are in the utmost vulnerable state that they can be in. This means that they are extremely impressionable and are looking for both a sense of belonging and a community.

This must be used to the puppy's advantage by showing them true care. Such true care means not smothering them with ridiculous levels of physical affection but by being somewhat affectionate while ensuring your puppy develops a progressive understanding of his/her place in the family. Routine is part of this understanding.

Should You Give Your Puppy Attention?

When your puppy arrives to his/her new house-hold, it is very important to know the difference between the right way and the wrong way to introduce him/her to the family and what is appropriate for this event. I wholeheartedly get that bringing your puppy home is a huge and defining moment for everyone. But the emotions are different for you and your puppy. For your young fluffy friend, there is an element of excitement and anticipation but there is also a lot of confusion, uncertainty and fear. For you, the same but you have the added advantage of planning and knowing how to manage the day. You must be aware that your puppy doesn't know why he/she is being taken away from his/her mother and siblings - you, on the other hand, do! Therefore, the onus is upon you to make absolutely sure that things run as smoothly as possible from the outset.

With all of the aforementioned advice in mind, you need to instruct your puppy of the rules in the correct manner. Straight away? Yes, absolutely! Puppies are impressionable and you need to lay down the ground work for a solid relationship between you and your fluffy companion.

So what's the first step?

Show the right amount of affection - not too much/too little

You heard me correctly. This can be hard because 'oh look how cute he/she is'. I get it - puppies are adorable **but** their appearance should not be a reason to let them off the hook with bad habits and behavior from the moment they arrive. When I say do not spend all your time with your puppy, what I mean is carry on with your day as you normally would. Don't make too many special provisions or plans that are out of the ordinary because that isn't a realistic picture of how you routinely will function in your day-to-day life.

Giving your puppy a sense of how things are going to be is a vital stepping stone to successful training and domestic adaptation. For example, if you're going to be out of the house and at work all day while he/she is all alone, then your puppy has to get used to that as soon as possible. Carry on as normal to prevent confusion or harmful over-attachment - in both parties.

The same applies if he/she exhibits vocal cries or moans. Do not automatically rush to their attention because this teaches him/her to be dependent and shows them that you will be there at every call. Trust me when I say that this method works. Puppies are far more independent and impressionable than human babies and as such, they pick up behavior patterns very quickly.

Another thing to ensure when you first get your dog, is that you are not strict or harsh with your puppy. Never raise your voice at him/her and do not scare or intimidate them. At such a young age, puppies are not trying to misbehave or do wrong. Their actions are based on natural urges for what feels right in their mind. Shouting at a puppy leads to trauma and a fragmented relationship with them. Do not do it!

On the contrast, demonstrate what behavior you do want to see. The best way to encourage this is to show him/her how to play with toys. Throw/squeeze/roll a toy and when your puppy chases after it, jumps, chews a toy or reacts playfully, stroke and/or cuddle him/her to establish a sense of achievement. This lets your puppy know that he/she did something that made you happy while feeling happy himself/herself. This is positive reinforcement and a healthy way to train your puppy from the first day.

On the first day, you will see acts of deviance from your puppy. Remember: he or she does not know any better yet so when you see him/her doing something bad such as jumping on a bed or chewing a pillow, say 'off!' with a firm but not strict voice and place one of his/her toys nearby to show him/her what they ought to be playing with/jumping on/chewing instead. Again, showing him/her praise and stroking him/her is essential for them to know they are doing the right thing.

A key thing to add to your day one to-do list is to find your local veterinary clinic and book an initial appointment. It is indispensable to ensure that a professional clinician talks you through vaccinations, dentistry and other healthcare which could crop up in the future. A side-note to this is to make sure you do not let your puppy outdoors until the vet gives a thumbs up.

--

First Introductions:
Your Puppy & The Family

Introducing your puppy to new people is one of the best parts of owning a puppy. Nonetheless, in the midst of all the delight, bear in mind that first introductions, particularly between your puppy and relatives/family members, when done right, are a crucial component of helping them to socialize (see the chapter on socialization for a more in-depth look at this). However, as reiterated, it must be done in the correct manner. Many families who adopt a puppy invite relatives round on the first day and so when the little one comes home for the first time, he is overwhelmed by the new faces, smells, excitement and sounds. It's a common feature for families to pass the puppy around from one person to the other.

Don't get me wrong - socialization and structure is a positive element of puppy training but you do need to give your puppy a few days to adjust to their surroundings. On the first and second days, ensure your puppy knows that **you** are its new owner(s) by being a pertinent (but not overbearing) presence in his/her life without the overwhelming hoard of people.

If your puppy is welcomed for the first time by a dozen new strangers (to him/her), he/she might think that you live in a pack and that these people will always be around. He/she might then become confused when they disappear home after a while.

Dogs make sense of their surroundings in a different way to humans. Humans make judgements based on a sort of mathematical sequence of logic. Canines assume permanence and will work out patterns in things based on their evolutionarily adapted cognitive abilities. I do encourage you to read the chapter on socialization which can be found later in this book and keep in mind the advice about properly socializing a puppy. It's a process that isn't instant but it is important that it happens from the second week (at the latest) and the second or third day (at the soonest)

2

Leashes and Leash Training

The topic of leashes can seem complicated, but it isn't when you learn what role they play in puppies and young dogs. A misconception which is common amongst new pet owners is that you can just pick up a small leash from a pet shop and use that on your puppy. This is a mistake! Leashes differ for adult dogs and puppies - it isn't a one size fits all concoction. Dog leashes are wide collared whereas puppy leashes are small and have a harness for bodily protection and placement.

Choosing the Right Leash

Choosing the right leash for your puppy depends mainly on what breed they are and their size. The best thing to do if you're unsure is speak to the attendant at your local pet store. Tell them that you need a harness leash for your puppy as well as what breed you have.

When selecting your leash, ensure you get the softest one you can find. Another erroneous belief some first-time puppy owners have is that softer leashes are more flimsy. Wrong! Softer harness-leashes provide maximum comfort. This matters not only because you want your puppy to feel safe but it's to make sure the puppy knows that you are not trying to harm him/her. Remember that puppies don't know what a leash or a harness is.

Once you choose the correct and most appropriate leash for your little one, it's time to get started on **leash training**. Getting this right from the get-go ensures success as your puppy grows out of puppyhood and into adulthood.

You might be wondering why there is a chapter dedicated to leash training - after all, isn't it simply a case of putting a leash on your young dog and allowing them time to get used to it?

In principle, yes! But the reality is, it takes many puppies a long time to figure out what a leash is for, so they tend to bite at it and more often, they'll tug and pull on it. Leash training is the process by which you teach your puppy that they need to be connected to you through the device for their own safety. It establishes a sense that you are in control and that they can't wander off at their own will.

When you first begin this form of training, your puppy will want to go where they please. They'll pull, against your movement and want to take over. Pulling on their leash is surprisingly common for puppies, especially very young ones. They do this because they feel pressure around their necks and it makes them very uncomfortable and scared. It's a new object to them and their canine instincts tell them that it's a threat to them as well as a nuisance.

When leash training, there are two important parts of this area of training - getting your dog used to the leash and helping them to walk on a leash. On the following page, I have laid out the best action plan for leash training your little puppy - bearing in mind maximum comfort and effectiveness.

Leash Training Success - Step by Step

- Ensure you buy a leash that also has a body harness. Bodily support reduces risk and helps your puppy keep their balance.

- Ensure leash is always loose and not tightened in any way.

- Be gentle and comforting when placing the mechanism on your puppy. Have treats and toys at hands if he/she gets stressed out.

- Once the harness and leash are on (loosely), stand up. Next, encourage your puppy to walk as normal. Do not move until your puppy is ahead of you. Make sure he/she is comfortable and not being tugged, even slightly. No pressure should be present apart from the extremely brief moment to change direction.

- When you feel your puppy pull or tug, tug very quickly to prevent it and then release the leash once more. It's important to enforce the idea that your puppy cannot pull at his/her will. This is important from a young age to instil into their minds.

Remember not to reward pulling and only give your puppy a treat when he/she obeys your movement and comes to you when he/she feels that (VERY BRIEF) split second tug. A tip that must be stated here is that you should purchase as soft a harness as you can find and only use harnesses during practice. Never leave it on. When your puppy grows older you can start introducing regular walking collars.

Ensure that all leashes you buy for your puppy come
with a harness.

3

How to Hold/Handle Your Puppy

Something which deserves its own chapter and is important to get right from day one is how to hold or rather, handle your puppy. This is essential for you to know as the puppy's owner(s) but relatives will also want to hold him/her and you must inform them of how to do it the right way. In this chapter, we will look at the various ways that you can hold and handle a puppy. We will then explore situations which may/will require you to handle your puppy and what to do in said circumstances.

When picking up a puppy, keep in mind that just like human infants, they get hurt much easier than we would. They are small, vulnerable and as such, you need to be as gentle as you can. Follow the step by step instructions on the following page to learn the correct way of picking up and handling your puppy. We will look at a few of the common ways you can hold your puppy.

Pick Up and Handle a Puppy

1. Start by positioning your hand just under the chest of your puppy. The ideal place is just by the rib-cage. If your puppy squirms, try under their forearm but ensure that your hand is steady and that you don't drop or hurt the puppy.

2. Their rear end needs equal support so as you pick your puppy up, quickly wrap your arm around their back legs and/or backside.

3. Now that your hands are positioned in the right fashion, lift up your puppy.

4. Bring the puppy close to your chest and support him/her accordingly.

- -

This is the most common method for picking up a puppy. Don't make too many movements when handling your puppy. Gently rubbing his/her head and comforting him/her will help relax your puppy.

When putting your puppy down, remember to do it right. **never** under any circumstance drop him/her deliberately and do not put him/her down suddenly. The best method is to lower him/her down to the ground. Bend down and ensure his/her paws have touched the ground before releasing them. Inform anyone who may handle your puppy on how to properly pick up, handle and set down the puppy.

Another method for picking up your puppy and holding him/her is to do it while they are in your lap. For this method, sit on the floor or on the bed. With your puppy in your lap, cuddle him/her and be playful with your approach. Rubbing the puppy's head softly makes this method the most effective. When he/she is completely relaxed, try turning your puppy over onto its back. This may not work straight away but if your puppy trusts you, it is made a lot easier. When and if you are able to turn them over successfully, you can now pick them up and handle them as outlined on the previous page. Now that we've gone over the ways you can pick your puppy up, it's time to talk about the times you'd need to apply this knowledge.

1. To be social.

The first and most obvious reason is to be social with your puppy. Your puppy loves affection and picking them up correctly can be part of a healthy bonding experience between you and your puppy.

2. When picking your puppy up from the vet.

When your puppy has been for a check up or vaccination or other veterinary procedure, you'll need to pick them up. It's important to note that if you're new to picking up and handling puppies, it's probably best to bring a crate with you or even a dog carrier. This is a question of safety and if you aren't confident yet with your handling skills, don't take any risks at the expense of your dog. A side note about carriers and crates is that you should always bring a blanket or two and have kibble or some other form of treat with you.

3. In an emergency.

In emergencies, knowing how to pick up and handle your dog is an absolute must-know! Of course in extreme emergencies where evacuations have to take place, it's most useful but in other emergencies puppy-handling is essential too. For example, if you're housetraining (see **chapter 5**) your puppy, you should be prepared to pick up your puppy to take him/her outside, especially if they have pooed or peed in the house.

4

Puppy Feeding 101: Food & Nutrition

This chapter is dedicated to what you need to know about feeding your puppy and all things food and nutrition. In the following section of this puppy training guide, we'll be exploring the following topics:

- What to feed your puppy.
- What not to feed your puppy.
- How much food you should give your puppy.
- The link between nutrition and exercise.
- Where you should & shouldn't feed your puppy.

1. What to feed your puppy.

Let's begin with what you need to know when it comes to the contents of your puppy's diet. You don't need a guide to tell you that your puppy is growing at a very fast rate. Within a year, they'll be adult sized dogs and as such, your role is to make sure thy maintain a healthy lifestyle and develop correctly.

In order to feed your puppy the correct food, you should opt for specialized puppy foods which you can pick up from pet stores. They have been specifically formulated for puppies and on the whole, they provide the best nutritional value for the price you pay. There are ways you can determine whether a puppy food is good or not. You should be looking for the following 3 qualities:

- High Protein
- Vitamin D, Calcium, Zinc and Magnesium
- High in Caloric Value

High protein and high calorie puppy foods are the best. They ensure proper organ and muscle growth & development (especially since your little one needs more calories than an adult dog). High nutrient content specifically of those mentioned above are crucial too - calcium and vitamin D are pivotal for bone health. Zinc and magnesium promote overall nerve health, immunity and gut health.

2. What not to feed your puppy.

There are some foods which you should flat out never feed your puppy! These can be toxic and fatal for dog consumption - especially during puppyhood. These foods include (but are not limited to):

- grapes
- chocolate
- onions
- shallots
- garlic cloves
- raw chicken
- raw beef
- raw fish
- peanuts
- candies
- avocado
- mushrooms

Always consult your healthcare professional (vet) before feeding your puppy anything that you are unsure about. It's never worth taking a risk.

3. How much food you should give your puppy.

It can be hard to determine how much you should feed your puppy. As a general outline, below is a guide to how much you should be feeding your little friend by age:

1-2 months old - 3 to 6 meals
2-3 months old - 4 to 5 meals
4-6 months old - 2 to 3 meals
6 moths and onwards - 2 to 3 meals

As with every advice for puppy feeding, quantity of meals per day depends on the breed and size of your dog.

4. The link between food and exercise.

Just like with humans and every other mammal, puppies use food for energy and therefore there is always a correlation between physical activity and food. As a general rule, don't feed your puppy immediately before they are scheduled to exercise. Likewise, don't feed them straight after activity either because this can cause a fatal twisting of the stomach known as severe gastric torsion. It's always best to wait until your puppy has rested for up to an hour before feeding him/her.

5. Where you should/shouldn't feed your puppy.

Something which isn't addressed enough in puppy related guides is the question of where you should feed your puppy. Your puppy should always be fed in places where they can enjoy privacy - typically away from noisy and busy places.

DO feed your puppy in:

- a quiet green space like your garden.

- a conservatory, if you have one.

- a place with a smooth surface that can be cleaned easily.

- a place away from children and other pets.

DON'T feed your puppy in:

- noisy and busy places.

- dirty places.

- a space surrounded by children.

- an area with dangerous concoctions.

- -

5

Housetraining/Housebreaking Your Puppy

You've probably worked out by now that your puppy is an in/out little machine when it comes to toilet habits. What you feed him/her seems to come out very quickly. I've met many puppy owners who are confused about why their puppy 'needs to go' so much and think they are doing something wrong. Not to worry - you aren't doing anything wrong and it's very normal for a puppy to have an uncontrolled and active bowel/bladder.

In this chapter, we will explore the most trouble-some area of puppy training and the main reason puppy owners have a hard time at the start - potty training or as we like to call it in the canine loving world - 'housetraining'. Housetraining isn't just a case of teaching your puppy where to go when they need the toilet, it's also about making sure your puppy goes from being wild with his/her toilet habits to being a well-trained young dog who understands the rules of the house and knows how to control their bladder - only using the allocated space for doing his/her business. It's a multifaceted area of training which you will have success in if you follow each step correctly.

Essentially, before and while your puppy is being housetrained, he/she must also be very aware of where he/she is allowed in the house and what is off limits. This sense of boundary might seem harsh but it's not - it's the most effective way that canines comprehend the limits and what they are/aren't allowed to do. As aforementioned a couple of times now, navigating a new environment can be arduous for puppies. They're new to your house and it's a lot bigger and more complicated than it would be for a human counterpart. As such, be considerate to the greatest extent possible and comprehend that it can take some puppies a lot of getting used to. They're living, sentient creatures and they are not deliberately trying to misbehave or frustrate you. For this reason, give them the benefit of the doubt if they slip up.

An initial note is that house-training a puppy can be very stressful and quite frustrating…well…*really* frustrating - but the good news is that all puppies get there eventually and in their own time. When they're young, puppies grow at a pretty rapid rate and thus, they eat more food since they require more energy. What's more is that since they haven't yet learned about controlling their bowel and bladder habits, it can seem like they are voiding themselves constantly.

As he/she learns how to develop their 'den' instinct - the instinct which tells them not to go when they are in the 'den' (household), training becomes easier. When they are amongst their mother and the rest of the litter, puppies are used to having the freedom to urinate and excrete wherever and whenever they desire. Housetraining concerns instilling limitations and showing them where they are permitted to do their business.

A common question is 'how long does it take to

housetrain a puppy'? Simply put, it depends but typically, they will not be fully housetrained until they're 6 months old since it takes 5-6 months for them to be able to fully control their bladder and bowel as well as fully understand what is expected of them during training.

Now it's time to get down to it.

How to Properly Housetrain a Puppy

The first step of housetraining is simple: you need to supervise your puppy to see how often and where they do their business. After you've worked out their habits, you need to quickly assert the rules. In fact, there are 6 vital rules when it comes to housetraining.

1. Choose a location for where your puppy's toilet area will be - usually a soil patch outside in a garden but in proximity to the house. This can be hard if you live in the city in an apartment or do not have access to outdoor spaces. In these instances, use a corner of the bathroom and set up a sort of litter box. Alternatively, an outdoor plant.
2. Allow them frequent (more than adult dogs) access to this area.

3. Use positive reinforcement (such as treats and toys) when your puppy successfully uses the toile area.

4. When you do work out your puppy's pattern,

develop a schedule for regular feeding and using the toilet area. This instills a sense of routine in your young dog (this is undoubtedly the most important rule).

5. For the first two to three weeks, keep a diary of your puppy's toilet habits.

6. Do not punish or scold your puppy when he/she is learning their routine. They will make mistakes so be level-headed.

- -

It is vital that you give your puppy time. As mentioned in the introduction, every puppy is different and some take longer/shorter to learn. A common question dog-owners ask vets and in online forums is why their dogs aren't learning faster. The time-frames in books and pamphlets are always rough guides. Some dogs can take much longer but as long as you love your puppy, your attitude during this process will determine everything.

I often get asked how often an average puppy goes. It isn't abnormal for a puppy to frequent the toilet every 30 to 50 minutes. This varies from food to dog and you also have to take into account the kind of chow you're feeding him/her and if they had treats. Also bear in mind how much/little water your puppy drank You'll be pleased to know that puppies sleep a lot and for a long period of time. They don't tend to need to pee or poop during this time.

While you are keeping a little diary of your puppy's schedule, also take one or two occasions in the night to ensure that your puppy is in his/her pen/crate/bed. Every dog owner can affirm that puppies love to wander about late at night. Keep an eye on them initially and make sure that they aren't getting themselves into unsafe mischief. If he/she is found wandering about or chewing the furniture, pick him/her up gently and with utmost care and place them back in their crate.

A top tip about housetraining is to feed your puppy regularly and at the same times. This speeds up the process because the in/output of food-excrement ratio will become routine pretty fast. Needless to say, always double-check that your puppy has sufficient amount of water in his/her bowl.

- -

How will I know when my puppy needs to go?

I desperately wanted to address this frequently asked question. It's true that in principle, you set up a designated area and your puppy goes to the toilet. But in reality- you just don't know when they need to because a dog will simply poop when he/she needs to often unprecedented. Even worse is when your puppy has their routine but on the way to using the toilet, they go on the floor half-way there.

Not to fret - there is a sure-fire way to handle this all-too-common scenario.

The solution is trial and error but will inevitably work. You have to work out when you fed your puppy. After 30 minutes (preferably just before, around 25 mins), take your puppy to his/her spot. Set them down. Wait for about five minutes and if your puppy doesn't need to go, leave it. Do this for a couple of days until they do go in the right place and make sure you give them as much praise as possible when this happens.

Rewarding a puppy lets them know 'oh I pooped where I was meant to' and they'll begin to associate pooping in that area with reward and pleasure. Believe me, they'll very quickly be more than willing to do their business their if a reward follows.

With time, your puppy will learn that their business must be done in one place. This creates a new dilemma. At night time, they'll start to cry, whine and howl calling you that they need the bathroom. When this happens, swiftly take them to their area and reward them once they're done. Put them straight back to bed.

Obviously, when they're older, they'll take the initiative to do this upon themselves. This process can take two to three months as bladder and bowel control does take time. They are learning so be patient but firm with the rules. Note that if you have a puppy of a larger breed of dog, use a loose leash to lead them to the toilet area.

I will also say that while pooping and needing to go is spontaneous in puppies, some do exhibit little warnings. These are usually circling a small area with their head down, sniffing excessively and low-level whining. Like human infants, you'll get to know your puppy pretty quickly and their behavior/personality etc.

A small but useful piece of advice to make your life easier when you're going to sleep is to bring your puppy to his/her toilet area just before you head to sleep. Sometimes he/she will need to go and other times not. However, giving them a chance to use the toilet before bed can save your sleep from being disturbed later in the night when your fluffy friend whines and howls.

What if I'm out and/or don't have time?

This is a common complaint among first time dog owners who have a busy life. The reality is, most of us have jobs to get to and lead lives that render us unable to be at our puppy's every beck and call. Not to worry, there is such a thing as 'passive dog training' or 'passive puppy training'. Whichever you like to call it, this involves house training them while you aren't around. The primary way to do this is to restrict your puppy to a puppy-proofed area of the house (preferably their toilet area). This gives them the freedom to go when they want and without your presence but it also instills in them the concept of knowing they can only go in a certain part of the house. If you choose this method, place the crate/pen, toys, food, water and everything he/she will need while you're out of the house.

The first couple of times you do this, it isn't uncommon for your puppy to shred up the paper, chew things and just be a little mischievous puppy. Don't get angry at him/her, this is completely normal. Once your puppy demonstrates knowledge of where to go and more stability, you can begin to introduce him/her to another puppy-proofed room of the house.

When people adopt puppies, there is a misconception that it is an easy process. It certainly isn't but it *is* rewarding! Consistency, patience and undying love for your dog are all the keys to successful training. Your puppy is a living and breathing animal so owners ought to expect that they'll be a handful at the start. This shouldn't sway owners from caring for and keeping a puppy because the love they will give you throughout their and your life cannot be underestimated.

Also, your puppy might not always show their appreciation for all you do but animal behaviorists have shown in their research that puppies do see **you** (the owner) in some way as his/her mother/father. They do have love for you but being responsible in these initial stages is so vital for your puppy to grow up to be the perfect companion and a happy and healthy dog.

6

Crating, Confinement and Adaptation

Learning independence is an important stage in the life of any dog or puppy - whether wild or domestic. Why? Because it teaches them to fend for themselves without relying on a dependent. This whole transition between dependence and independence is a part of what we call **crate training**.

You might be wondering what in the world crate training is.

Crate Training :
(definition)

Crate training is where you train your puppy or dog to associate their crate/cage as a safe space or safe location.

This is especially important as they begin to develop their 'den' instinct which all dogs possess. Crate training isn't easy - that much ought to be emphasized from the get-go but with persistence it can be a good way to help your puppy navigate their new house before they're ready to roam free.

Crate training can take up to 4 weeks although most puppies can be successfully trained within 2 to 3 weeks. Again, it all depends on the temperament, personality and playfulness of your puppy. What I will say from the start is that crate training is TEMPORARY and should not be a way of imprisoning your dog or restricting them for long periods of time. This borders into cruelty and so it is so key to get it right if you are going to use the crate approach.

Until puppies are fully house-trained, they should not be able to roam about as they please throughout the household. Not only is this a health and safety issue for your pup, but it's also so that they learn that they cannot pee and poop where they please. The last thing you want is to be cleaning your house of mess all the while having a disobedient puppy.

Before we get to how to crate train, I will note that there is an alternative to this method. Some owners prefer confinement training. This was briefly touched upon earlier but to elaborate, confinement training is where you limit a puppy's access to a puppy-proofed room of the house where he/she has everything he/she needs. Utility rooms, well-sized conservatories and kitchen areas are the best.

In both confinement and crate training, you are not keeping the puppy captive and you must ensure that all their needs are met. Positive reinforcement albeit with toys, kisses, cuddles, treats or otherwise is essential in both - regardless of which one you try.

So now that this distinction has been clarified, let us talk about what crate training involves. Confining him/her to a conservatory (for instance) is an effective way to housetrain your puppy and aids them in understanding their limits on where to pee and poop. It moreover signifies to them that they are not permitted to use the rest of the house as a toilet area.

The main purpose of crate training is to discourage your puppy from peeing or pooping when in confined spaces so that they will be encouraged to do so when let out. In this process, he/she will learn to find the designated toilet area which you have set out for them. Another benefit of crate training is that it teaches them to control their bladder and bowel.

I cannot state clearly enough that the crate method is temporary and you should not exceed two hours of it. It can have detrimental effects otherwise. Unlike confinement which provides your puppy with everything he/she needs for a long period of time while you're out, crate training should only be performed under your presence and supervision for a short period.

So how do I crate train my puppy, the right way?

It's very simple - let your puppy out every hour and take him/her to their toilet area. Once there, allow them up to ten minutes to use the space for their business. For whatever reason, if he/she doesn't need to go, just repeat the process and during the occasions that he/she does do his/her business, reward them appropriately. If your puppy is especially young, do keep them in the crate for longer than 30-50 minutes.

Just like I said earlier, keep a diary of how your puppy is getting along. This not only helps to keep track of progress but can prove to be an invaluable record if your vet ever asks about your puppy's bowel/bladder habits. Mistakes can and do occur during crate training, so as always, be patient and consistent when things don't go to plan.

7

Puppy Emotions and Mental Well Being

The mental state of your puppy is something that you should see as a priority. Puppies, just like all young mammals, are emotionally complicated. They have varied needs and sometimes, it's not always obvious what the problem is. Luckily, puppies do exhibit outwardly what they feel inwardly. Whether it's loneliness, distress, boredom, pain or need for exercise, understanding why your puppy is feeling the way that he/she is, is important.

What will be explored in this chapter, is how you can identify and manage common behavioural issues that your puppy might face. We'll look at the two categories of behavioral management : destructive and traumatic. The so-called destructive category consists of biting, scratching and disobedience. The traumatic one is made up of crying, whining and howling.

Biting/Nipping

Ouch! My puppy likes to nip/bite. What should I do?

The first and most prevalent typical puppy behavioral action is **biting/nipping**. Aside from whining, crying and howling, puppies, especially while their teeth are coming through, puppies love to nip. It's very normal and most dogs grow out of it because their mother teaches them against it at a young age. A lot of owners begin to worry about nipping and biting, especially if it persists. It's especially common as a behavior in puppies between the ages of five and eighteen months.

If you have a particularly young puppy, it is thought of to be especially important to train them not to nip/bite before the 8 month mark. However, before we look at solutions and how to get your puppy to quit biting and nipping, it's vital to comprehend why puppies take up nipping to begin with.

There are often two primary reasons why a young dog is prone to nipping:

(a) social isolation and fear.

Some puppies can feel intense loneliness, especially when new to a family, owner and/or household. In some instances, this develops into what dog-experts call 'fearful aggression'. In this frightful time for your puppy, he/she likes to use biting as a way to try and scare people/other dogs off when they are afraid. However, this is the least likely reason why dogs specifically nip. Puppies are highly sociable and cases of biting caused by fear and isolation are typically more common in puppies with trauma or who witnessed trauma (often in their mothers).

Aside from fear, lack of socializing with other humans and dogs causes them to bite too. Since they were taken away from their sisters and brothers of their mother's litter, it's up to you to ensure they get adequate time with their own species and are socialized with people the correct way too. More on this later.

Another reason why a puppy will bite is if they dislike you, perceive you as a threat or do not respect you as an authority figure. Just like any dog owner will confirm, trust and respect are essential for your relationship with your dog. You must take it upon yourself to respect your puppy and in turn they will respect you. This applies to discipline as well. As aforementioned, positive reinforcement, rewards and affection are essential for your puppy's respect for you. If you are too stern like many bad owners are, your dog will not respect you and will resent you forever. Scolding never works so do not do it! Whenever you are training your puppy, make sure your love for them is visible. With vocal reprimands when you tell them off, it must be followed by a reward when they do the right thing.

(b) overexcitement

The most common reason that puppies nip, is from overexcitement. While excitement can be cute and a sign of a positive and happy-go-lucky puppy, too much of it can become a hinderance in training and can become a burden pretty fast! Why? Because when excited, puppies nip and sometimes pee uncontrollably. The best way to avoid the onset of overexcitement is to make sure that your dog is getting sufficient playtime, social time and outdoor time.

So now that we know the reasons why puppies nip, we need to address solutions to the problem. What you need to know as a puppy owner is that as soon as your puppy starts to nip, you need to be decisive at once! You can either stop playing with him/her immediately or alternatively withdraw from the puppy as soon as possible (this is the puppy equivalent of a 'time out'). Once you've ceased the activity, you need to calm your pup down. The most effective way of doing this is to take your puppy away from whatever was getting him/her overexcited and stimulated to begin with and prevent further excitement from happening. A crate is an ideal place to put your puppy. Only isolate your puppy for a short period of time - ten minutes usually does the job.

Doing this several times when your puppy starts to bite and nip ensures that he/she understands that you are not pleased with that behavior. While your pup will undoubtedly grow out of this habit, stopping it from the earliest point possible is a great course of action to prevent future mishaps.

Socialization

It's time to talk about socializing your puppy correctly. Dogs are social creatures - this means that they have hierarchies within their packs. Just like humans, social animals need to interact with others for optimal mental health. Isolation leads to horrible consequences like biting, uncontrolled barking and aggression.

Puppyhood is therefore the best time to start your little friend on their social adventures. It is believed that the best duration for social training is 3-4 months although socialization has to be an ongoing process thereafter. You may begin this process from the day you get your puppy.

How to Successfully Socialize Your Puppy

1. Encourage friends and family members to meet your puppy. Your puppy needs to become acquainted to new people, smells and personalities.

2. Safely bring your puppy to social events, the mall, shopping, school events if you have children and so on.

3. Take your puppy on car rides.

4. Once house-trained, let your puppy explore items of clothing, bags, boxes and so on where new experiences, smells and textures can become a part of their sensory experience.

5. Encourage friends who have pets to meet your puppy, even if they aren't dogs!

6. Don't hesitate to vacuum around your puppy: he/she needs to become used to sounds of the human world.

7. Let your puppy explore leashes, collars and so on so that they become used to different objects.

- -

With all of these tips, I will state that you should expect your puppy to be frightened and uncomfortable at times. This is normal and if they are especially afraid, wait a few days and try the activity again.

Howling and Whining

On the other side of troublesome puppy behavior, we have the auditory issues that make themselves manifest through howling and whining. As a first time dog owner it can be hard to know what your puppy is trying to tell you.

We'll now explore this common problem to help you navigate the principle reasons why your puppy is so vocal and the psychological implications of the messages they convey in this manner. After this has been established, you'll be taken through the steps on what to do and what not to do.

Puppies whine and cry. This is a fact for 99 if not 100 per cent of young dogs. The most common reason is fear which is why you might notice that your puppy cries most when he/she is isolated and alone. Remember that when puppies are taken from their mothers, they can be traumatized. This is why it's important to reassure them and make sure they know that they're safe. Much like wolves, puppies will whine and howl when alone. In the wild, canines do this when abandoned. It's therefore normal but more often than not, puppy owners who aren't used to this worry that something is horribly wrong. This is especially the case in breeds that produce very loud cries. Not to worry though, we'll guide you through what you need to know.

The harsh reality is that you need to train your young dog that isolation and being alone in general are natural parts of life and so, in the first instance, unless it's late at night and your dog needs the toilet, you should not answer and rush in every time they cry. This applies when you're around the house and you hear her/him cry. Do not instinctively give them attention because they need the tough love of being on their own sometimes. In nature, it would be the same thing. If a young dog cries out, not every cry will be answered. This is important so that your puppy can develop a healthy relationship to you, other people and other dogs (this will be covered later on).

A significant reason why you shouldn't give your puppy attention every time he/she cries is because they will begin to learn that you will always be there and this can create a sense of control over you in his/her mind. This isn't good because otherwise you could very feasibly have a badly behaved puppy on your hands.

Other than fear and loneliness, puppies whine and howl when they aren't used to their environment/crate/house/pen yet. In instances where you've given your puppy space and he/she still whines after a week or 10 days, then do spend a little more time with him/her than you usually would. If after you've tried this for three days and he/she still whines, it's time to be a little bit stern. When you leave and he/she carries on crying, assert firm but not harsh dominance with a shout. Usually this is the word 'no!' said abruptly but some owners shout 'hey!' or 'shush!'. If he/she quietens after a few minutes, praise your puppy and cuddle him/her. They need positive reassurance when they have behaved well. You certainly don't want your puppy thinking you don't love them or that they aren't wanted.

They will also begin associating your departures with privacy and will quickly become accustomed to the idea of being alone sometimes. The good thing is that they know you'll return which provides comfort in their minds.

Many puppy owners believe that the second their puppy begins crying, they have to act. This is wrong. Always give him/her the benefit of the doubt and allow them to cry/whine for a short time. When you hear your puppy being vocal, just wait a few moments. If he/she persists, assume that he/she needs the toilet. If this turns out not to be the case, bear in mind the steps on the previous two pages.

Also keep in mind that your puppy might just be reacting to an environmental change. It isn't uncommon for a puppy to cry if he/she is cold, hungry or even thirsty. If you have other pets, your puppy might be afraid of them at first. Use rationale first before assuming anything about your puppy. They are complex, just like we are.

With regards to puppies who are attention-seeking which is common also, remember not to necessarily give in to them and never praise them when they've been badly behaved. It's always best to give them space and a non-harsh but firm command. At the same time, you shouldn't let your puppy feel too lonely. Abandonment can be hard so they need some affection from you - more as they become house trained fully!

I still can't work out why my puppy is crying!

I've heard this one a million times and truthfully speaking, yes, puppies do whine for no reason sometimes and it can be difficult to know what to do when you've tried everything to settle them and comfort them.

Canines love to vocalize - it's what they do and especially at a young and vulnerable age, their whines can be uncontrolled and constant. While they seemingly whine for no reason, it's only 'no reason' from a human perspective. Usually, they have a reason but it's very challenging to work it out when it isn't hunger, loneliness, thirst, feeling uncomfortable or needing the toilet.

In such instances, rule out as many possibilities as possible. If you have and you're still confused, the reality could be that your puppy has learned a bad habit. In most cases of dogs that I've worked with, excessive crying, howling or whining is the result of bad training. These puppies have learned that they can get what they want by whining. This results from owners who gave them way too much attention, owners who gave them too many treats, owners who let their puppies get away with everything, owners who did not give their puppies space or any sort of vocal reprimand and so on.

It's hard to get your puppy to unlearn this but instant action is needed. The best solution for young puppies is just to start re-training them into good housetraining habits. If your puppy is getting older and more mature, retraining can be very arduous, to say the least. In this case, you'll need to change their routine a bit. A great way to get them to stop whinging all the time is to let them get more exercise every day, and putting them on socialization programs with other dogs can work wonders! While keeping your puppy more busy than usual, start to distance yourself a little bit from them since it's likely they are used to being the center of attention. Again, use the firm 'no!' to teach them about independence. A balance of care and isolation is what you must aim for. Not abandonment nor over-affection!

When you succeed with handling your puppy's whining habits, it's important to keep an eye on them. If for whatever reason, after a month or so, your dog exhibits unusual crying, a health problem could be to blame. It's therefore essential to get them to their vet as soon as possible!

Raiding, Invading and Other Mischief

Your puppy **will** get up to some mischief! This is a given and all puppy owners know this. Among the most routine bad habits that puppies exhibit inside the home, is raiding the bin or just about any container that contains possible food. In the mind of your pup, the bin is a seemingly fantastic source for treats and while we wish there was a sure-fire solution to teach dogs against raiding the bin, this is unfortunately not plausible. While not the solution you may have hoped to hear, the only way to stop your young dog from bin raiding, is to move the bin to a location your dog can't reach.

Faecal Consumption

First time puppy owners (especially labrador owners) are often grossed out and mortified when they find out that their dog is eating his/her own poop. Some even report confusion as to why their other dogs aren't doing it, just their dog! Well, in all honesty, many puppies - particularly sporting dogs such as labradors have a tendency to indulge in this kind of behavior.

Why?

For many decades, the main reasons were only theorized but the principle and overwhelming evidence suggests that dogs consume their own faeces either because of neutering or because of underlying health issues that make them extremely hungry to the point of eating whatever they can get their paws on. In the first instance, it seems like the lack of sex hormones drives some dogs to eating their own poop. Studies have shown this behavior is frequent in female young dogs but are still not sure why it occurs. In the case of health issues, some disorders of the bowel as well as diabetes can render a dog famished as nutrients are not well absorbed. So, they end up eating faeces because they are simply over-hungry!

In puppies however, it's a different (and less concerning) story. Puppies (especially lab puppies) who eat their own faeces do so as a habit which they eventually grow out of. They often taste their faeces thinking it has some kind of nutrition to it and either never do it again or acquire a taste for it. They grow out of this in almost every instance. In any case, if you are concerned about your puppy's consumption of their own poop and think there is an underlying issue, seek the advice of your local vet but do bear in mind how common it is for puppies to engage in this kind of behavior.

8

All About Obedience

This chapter will cover obedience training which can be challenging if you aren't too sure where to begin. For the sake of simplicity, this chapter will be broken down into the various aspects of obedience and discipline.

Successful Obedience and Discipline

We will first address obedience and discipline which will feed nicely into the next two parts of this chapter. Obedience training is a core element of puppy training but it does not necessarily prevent all emotional issues in young dogs. What obedience training is particularly useful for is enabling a central sense of communication between your puppy and you.

While it sounds relatively harsh, obedience training is simply the term used to describe when you want to teach your dog to do something. This can be anything from sitting to fetching and even staying still and calm in stressful situations. We spoke about social structures in canines in the chapter 'Day Four' but obedience training helps to develop a sense of social structure in the household between your dog and his/her owner(s) i.e. you.

The rewarding aspect of obedience training is that when your puppy listens and obeys you, it means that he/she is demonstrating clear love and respect for you. Compliance is what you want out of the exercise. However, it isn't a question of rendering your dog scared - not at all - in fact this would be counter-intuitive. Instead, obedience training draws a line between you, the dog's carer, and your puppy who is subordinate in the structure of the household. Teaching your puppy or young dog tricks such as raising their paws when you raise your hand playfully can work wonders and dogs actually like learning this form of communication. It is a healthy way to show submission to you.

All in all, obedience training should be light-heart-ed and an effective way of bonding with your puppy. A common thing that people say is that you can't train a puppy! This is a misconception and in my ex-perience with dogs, puppies can and do learn effec-tive means of communication during this sort of training. To say that a puppy cannot learn obedience is to say that they have no personality and awareness. This is completely wrong since they have a lot of both. I believe as do many, that the earlier you start training a dog, the better. Their behavior isn't always going to be predictable so the younger you start training them, the better the chances are for long term success.

For obedience training, I would highly suggest that you research training centres and classes in your local area. Trained professionals can work wonders for your puppy and it's also a beneficial social experi-ence for them. You don't need to send your puppy to more than a couple of classes but it is suggested by many vets and carers that puppies do attend one or two classes for the basics. The rest can be done by you at home.

So, how do I start?

You start obedience training wherever you want. It's best if it's outdoors and in the so-called 'real world' because while there are distractions, your dog needs to get used to them as quickly as possible. Obedience training is really down to you. Whether that's gently lifting their paw and saying a catch-word which identifies it over and over until they associate the sound and movement with the action or whether it's teaching them to sit and stay, it's up to you.

A common obedience training method is car obedience whereby you help your dog to practice staying calm and seated in your car. Remember not to actually drive during training. Let your dog become accustomed to the space, smell, and environment of the vehicle. After a few minutes of initial sniffing, exploration and intrigue, your puppy will settle down and that's when you can take them inside and do the same thing five or six times before practicing driving with them in the car. Start with small, safe and local trips and if your puppy starts to whine or get excited, vocal reprimanding can be enforced aiding in car obedience training.

You're probably sick of hearing this but reward is the important part of obedience training. Do not fail in showing your puppy contentment and praise when he/she stays, sits, fetches or other actions. They deserve it and they will know how to act in accordance to your rules from then on.

Calling and Name Recognition

Name recognition is a frequently discussed subject in the world of puppy ownership. Owners have trouble choosing a name and also in enforcing the name when getting the puppy to recognize those instances when he/she has been addressed directly.

To most puppies, hearing their name or being called helps to register in their minds as 'time to run' and so they scurry away from you. This is because they identify commands with being pushed to do something or with discipline and/or danger or threat. This must be reversed and is a more advanced part of training.

Here, we will talk about getting your puppy to recognize not only when they are being called but to actually approach and respond to their name. Before telling you all about what you should do, it's key that we cover what not to do (the things that a lot of owners don't realize they are doing wrong).

One of the most terrible things you can do as an owner when training your young puppy to come to you at the command of their name, is to allow them off their leash - especially in public. Many owners erroneously believe that it's completely fine to let their dogs run free without their leash and do other things that do not involve the owner. In doing this, you are telling your puppy that 'fun' and 'exercise' are things that do not involve you. As such, they will not associate you with that pleasurable sentiment and freedom. Moreover, when it comes time to go home, you put the dog back on the leash and suddenly, YOU'RE the bad guy because in their minds, you've ended the good time they were enjoying. This can be troublesome for your relationship with your young dog and can lead to unwanted tension and disrespectful behavior on their part.

What you're also informing your puppy is that it's much more worthwhile to disobey than to end the fun. So what can you do as an owner to get your dog to come when called and respond to their name?

Quite simply, you need to instil within his/her mind that being called is not a bad thing. They need to associate you and your demand of their presence as something positive for them. Dogs are intuitive, as I've stated a few time already and something unique to puppies is that they are constantly trying to work out when we are instructing them and when we are being passive with them. The ideal situation in calling your dog is if they identify pleasure with your presence when you want them and they acknowledge that they're being instructed. Another scenario you do not want is upon successfully teaching your puppy to come to you but they think it is a punishment. A lot of owners do manage to get their dogs to come to them but only to clip their nails, give them a bath or something else unpleasant for the dog's wishes. You will need to do these things of course, but in the first few weeks and months, when calling your dog and getting his/her attention, it's best to play with them, give them treats, cuddles, toys, kisses and so on. Nothing demanding or taxing for them.

Let them want to come when called because of this association with pleasure and fun. Eventually, they'll understand that being called is an act of love from you to them.

I will once more put onus on how great behavior and obedience classes can be for young dogs and it will save you a lot of stress in the long run. After one or two sessions, you should aim for 10 to 15 minutes a day of calling training. It does get easier with time though. It's pushing through these initial stages and laying down a good foundation that requires some effort.

I now want to take you through practical steps for perfect 'Coming When Called' training.

- -

Coming When Called

1. Preparation

Just like any element of young dog and puppy training, preparation is everything. Step one is to ensure your puppy actually wants to learn and isn't tired.

At meal time, take a treat or piece of food and place it near your puppy's nose. If he/she does not respond, try waving it gently. If he/she is still not interested, come back later and try another time. When your puppy is ready and does show interest to the food, it's time for training.

2. Secrets to Getting a Puppy's Attention

Now that you're ready and your puppy is too, feed your puppy a limited amount of food from your hand - not more than two or three pieces of chow or kibble. Inevitably, your dog will want more if he/she is hungry.

Step back a little bit with food in your hand and watch as your puppy is intrigued and wants the food. Say 'here girl/here boy! Come here!' or something of the same iteration. Stretch your food hand out towards his/her nose and your dog should approach. If he/she does, reward her with praise and cuddles. Give them the food right away. This ensures they know they'll be rewarded in this 'little so-called game'.

Next, lower yourself to your puppy's level while

simultaneously holding their collar gently. They'll get the message and when they approach closer, give them more food.

It is recommended that you repeat this exercise every day until it becomes natural. The same principles of this exercise can be applied to calling your dog over to play but instead of food, the reward is a ball/toy/treat/cuddles.

When your puppy gets the hang of the food calling training, you'll need to progressively decrease the food rewards but keep the same 'come to me' principle in mind. For the best training, rewards should not be given every time. Only when he/she comes especially quickly and in a direct manner. This means your dog doesn't take advantage of your kindness or the situation on the whole.

Coping With Excitement

It's time to talk about something that every puppy owner can attest to - excitement. While excitement can be cute and a sign of a positive and happy-go-lucky puppy, too much of it can become a hinderance in training and can become a burden pretty fast! Why? Because when excited, some puppies urinate uncontrollably and chew excessively as well.

If your puppy training experience is going well but you're still finding the odd puddle of urine here and there or your puppy still likes to chew when happy, it's time for a specialized action plan.

Firstly, we must appreciate that puppies who do pee when excited often have bladder control issues and in these puppies, it's just a question of you needing to housetrain your puppy for a bit longer than expected until it stops. Your puppy doesn't necessarily know he/she is doing anything wrong so do not reprimand harshly.

If his/her bladder is under control and you're still having issues with an over-excited puppy who urinates around the house, you may simply need to ensure that he/she doesn't get himself/herself in an over-excited state to begin with. The best sure-fire way to do this is to make sure they are getting sufficient playtime, social time and outdoor time. Let them go crazy during these times so that they won't feel the need to be over-excited when inside the house.

Many owners complain that their dog urinates when they return home or someone new arrives at the house. In these cases, it's always best to ignore your puppy. Ignore them up to five times until they get bored and realize that you aren't interested in their over-excitement. Remember : DOGS LOVE ROUTINE and this helps them a great deal with understanding boundaries - and it helps you in not having to clean up as much pee.

Play is very important - especially with the owner present.

Barking and Howling

Earlier, we delved into coping with a puppy who whines and cries. As time goes on though, dogs vocalize through barking.

You don't say!

As a puppy or young dog owner, I'm sorry to tell you this but you'd better start getting used to the fact that your puppy will bark. It's just what they do. I've met dog owners who complain about barking but many fail to bear in mind that telling a dog not to bark is like telling a human not to talk. However, barking and howling does become a problem when it's excessive. Dogs know that they can communicate emotions vocally - and they do use their vocal capacities to do so. In this segment, we'll look at why excessive barking occurs and how to control it. That way, you won't have those annoying neighbors knocking on your door at all hours in the night.

The first kind of problem barking occurs in dogs who feel like they need to 'let out' or release energy which is pent-up. A lot of these dogs do feel confined and somewhat lonely. So, the first thing to assume if you have a barking dog is to add extra outdoors and play time to the schedule. Allow them to exercise more and release tension which has undoubtedly built up for a while.

In fact, you'll want to do this as soon as possible because many dogs begin to enjoy barking and use it as a substitute to physical exertion. This is a huge problem so make sure it doesn't get to this stage by letting your dog out (on a leash) more than once a day or until their barking reduces to a normal amount.

Alternatively, your dog might bark as much as they do because you accidentally conditioned them that way. You might be wondering what I'm talking about. As a young puppy, some owners respond to every one of their dog's whines and howls with a treat or with a response. Your dog might have ingrained in their brain that they can control you this way and talk to you using the mechanism which seems to have worked until now.

How do I get my dog to bark less?

What you must do in the first instance is cure the underlying cause of barking. As aforementioned, this is most likely to be a lack of exercise or intense emotion (boredom, fear and so on). Obedience training is another solid solution as there are many professionals trained in this area. If you opt out of this, I would suggest you spend more time with your dog because it could just be a case of lack of attention. Too much and too little attention are detrimental to your dog's overall mental well-being.

In cases where your dog does get sufficient exercise and outdoors time, perhaps he/she is in desperate need of socialization - albeit with other dogs or people. Dogs get lonely and some do bark in excess when isolated from others. A quick solution is to spend time with him/her and also to go on a walk with him/her on a leash. Roaming the neighborhood after work hours or on a Sunday can provide your dog with great little social adventures of meeting new people. Dogs love to be the center of attention and they know when people find them cute. Help them to boost their ego and let them revel in the moment.

Just as important as outdoor time and socializing is feeling a sense of belonging. If you work long hours and your dog is home alone for a lot of the day, he/she might not feel a part of the family unit. Play games with him/her more often, give her more love, cuddle with her/him while on the couch and just integrate your dog into more everyday parts of your family life.

*Can I teach my dog to **stop** barking?*

To an extent, yes!

Believe it or not, unless told to do so, dogs aren't aware that their barking causes you or anyone else a problem. If they did, it would be much simpler to get them to stop barking or to reduce how much they bark. Therefore, you need to learn how to train your dog that barking is not a good thing and that it is in fact a nuisance.

Establish this rule for your dog :

It's okay for you to bark until you are told to stop!

Just like every other obedience command, telling your dog to stop barking is a command of instruction. Do not get it confused with a reprimand such as 'no!' or 'off!'

The way it works is as follows. Every time you hear your dog barking, allow two barks. If he/she continues, use the command 'stop barking boy/girl!' When doing this, have a treat at hand that she/he can smell/see. The magic here is that your dog will undoubtedly stop barking because they'll be far too fascinated by what you have for them. They'll sniff the treat and likely eat it.

Now what will happen is he/she will be distracted for a while but nine times out of ten, he/she will bark again soon. When he/she does, bring another treat in front of him/her but do not let him/her have it right away. Wait ten seconds until he/she is completely quiet and willing to take it. She/he will eventually catch on to the fact that staying quiet = yummy treats and this tends to work rather quickly.

Be patient. It might require three to five times of trying before your dog understands what is being asked of him/her. The idea is to get him/her to understand that not barking means that he/she gets rewarded. After a short while, they'll willingly do this without much prompting. Do keep in mind that dogs do use barking as a mechanism of communication so even if after a while of your dog being trained he/ she barks abnormally, suspect that there is a health problem and take him/her to the vet. Especially in younger dogs but older ones too. It's never a good idea to push back vet visits - don't take the risk.

Separation and Isolation Anxiety

A common behavioral pattern exhibited by puppies is separation/isolation anxiety. Unfortunately, people are quick to blame the owners for puppies who cannot detach emotionally from them - this is a misconception. Puppies do not like to be alone, this is a fact. Some experience higher than normal levels of sadness and anxiety when you do leave them alone though. They demonstrate these emotions clearly and in destructive ways - crying, biting, chewing things and urination.

When your puppy is showing signs of isolation and not wanting to be left alone, it is vital that you occupy them with new things. In their minds, the world is limited to you, food and treats. Expose them to more toys and allow them to play with/be interested by new obstacles through play. Balls, stuffed cubes and noisy toys tend to work best - in my experience of owning and looking after puppies. Another great way of keeping them occupied is to introduce them to other puppies at designated play areas (on the Meetup app, these exist in big cities and some towns). Alternatively, if feasible, get another pet to keep them occupied but this is just a suggestion.

In addition to adding more toys to their little life, plan time that is just dedicated to playing with them. It helps if there is more than one of you (a partner, friend, relative, child etc). Puppies like to be stimulated and it helps their excitement and overall happiness.

Puppies that Jump

A final area of puppy training that I want to address is jumping - something that is common in almost all puppies. Puppies are social - very social actually - especially when you compare them to the young of other mammalian pets. As such, they love to show us affection and a well-known way young dogs do this is by jumping on us. How many times have you been in a park or taking a walk and a happy dog has sniffed, licked or jumped up at you? Chances are, quite a few!

Puppies do get particularly excited and it's a big deal for them when they get the opportunity to exhibit their anticipation and happiness for someone with affection. Jumping is a mechanism they use to expel that energy is a vivid manner. It's a form of greeting in all dogs. Just to clear something up - puppies, when very young, will usually waddle to you and lick but as they get older, jumping does become a habit.

While jumping is usually fine and needs no training or discouragement, there are times when jumping becomes immoderate and happens too often. Excessive jumping can be dangerous if there are young children or senior citizens around.

When dogs jump, they also pounce and have a quick wit about the execution of the landing. This can be a problem and somewhat burdensome.

So why do some dogs jump and pounce all the time?

You might find this hard to believe but actually, it is us, the owner(s) who is to blame! The way we raise puppies is the problem, to be more specific. Let me explain. When a puppy is young, we bend down to lower ourselves to them. As they start to grow and learn to be more effective jumpers, we give in and find is more simple to just let them come up to our level with the famous jump-greet.

Who can blame us though - we walk upright on two legs. But even if we can't help it, we condition dogs to come up to our level instead of taking it upon ourselves to consistently lower ourselves to theirs.

What makes this habit worse is how enthusiastic *we* are when we allow our dogs to jump on us. This tells the dog that it's completely acceptable for him/her to do this. Not only are we passively accepting it, but in the minds of our beloved fluffy friend, we are endorsing it wholeheartedly.

Therefore, think how confusing it must be for a puppy or young dog when you OUT OF THE BLUE tell them that it's not okay to do the thing you essentially trained them to do when greeting you. Most of the time, they'll ignore your sudden disapproval and continue doing it.

Solving the problem of a jumpy dog or puppy does not constitute of unlearning the habit, but rather, teaching them a new and better means of greeting you and other humans.

The most effective way is to teach him/her to stay and to sit/stay put when they do jump up. It'll take time but be persistent. The first step is to start lowering yourself to them for cuddles and kisses. Get yourself and your dog into this habit. Encourage visitors to your house to do the same thing and don't take no for an answer. If your puppy or dog doesn't listen to you and continues to jump on the person, pull your dog off of them and firmly assert a reprimand like 'no!' or 'off, now!'

Consistency is important as with all training that has been covered but with this particular kind of training, it is re-training. This means it's harder for your dog to learn and to be consistent in. You are undoing a natural habit which they were previously accustomed to. It's crucial to stick at it every day until you see improvements.

9

Puppy Training FAQs

We've now covered the essentials of puppy training with focus on the practical side of things. The aim of this section is to help you navigate common problematic areas by answering the most frequently asked puppy training questions. It's easy to feel lost and uncertain when it comes to making the best decisions for your puppy. There is a lot to keep in mind when talking about puppy care, so instead of throwing random questions into the mix, the following FAQs have been organized by category. There will be 3 which include **food & nutrition**, **leashes**, and **housetraining**. After, there will be a section which is dedicated to more general puppy questions. Ones which can help you if you are still in the process of choosing a puppy or even if you're deciding whether or not to get one. Without <u>fur</u>ther ado (pun intended), let's get straight into it...

- -

Food and Nutrition

Q. What is the best diet for my puppy? What are the best food brands?

It's understandable in an over-commercialized world to not know what the best brand of food is for your puppy! There are many great ones and on the specifics of the branding, I'm not going to offer any advice for obvious reasons. However, you should always talk to your vet about forming a diet around your dog's needs and breed. Your vet will be able to give you breed and body specific info about home made treats, semi moist & tinned food, including dry foods and so on. In any case, contrary to popular belief, you should not create diversity in your puppy's diet. That is, you should stick to food and food brands that you know your little pup can stomach well without any stomach upset.

Q. How often should I feed my puppy?

Since puppies are constantly growing, you need to

ensure that they are eating regularly - 4-5 times a day if they are under 5 months old and 3-4 times thereon. Whenever you feed your puppy, ensure plenty of water is available. I can't overstate this!

Q. What treat(s) should I choose for my puppy?

It's always a good idea by principle to select a small treat which is both low in calories (kcal content) and enjoyable. Remember that treats are for when your puppy has done something good and so they need to associate it with pleasure and reward. If you're being careful about your puppy's daily calorie content, make sure you count their treat in with their daily amount.

Leashes

Q. Which leash is the best for my puppy?

This question has been answered to an extent in the chapter dedicated to all things related to leashed and leash training but I wanted to talk about more specific elements of choosing the ideal leash for your puppy, especially if you want very precise info concerning the ideal leash. My first tip would be to go for a **nylon** leash. They are softer and come in all sorts of colors, sizes and even textures. All in all, nylon is the ideal material for puppy leashes because of their general softness and also the fact that they won't cause leash burn in puppies. When your puppy gets older, especially if you have a dog from a fast-growing breed, like labradors, it's important to stop using nylon leashes and these are less suitable for adult dogs in general.

With regards to durability, you want to choose a good high quality leash that is going to last you without breaking or causing any havoc. If nylon isn't your thing, leather is a good alternative. They have a great grip and soften with use making it ideal for a puppy to use. A lot of puppy owners opt for cheaper leashes which are typically chain leashes. However, don't fall into that trap! They break easily and you'll find yourself dishing out more money in the long-term as you'll keep needing to replace them.

A final tip with regards to the material of a leash for your puppy is investing in a cotton leash.

A cotton leash?! What's that?

While very difficult to find unless you scavenge the internet for a highly reputable leash/puppy supplies company, cotton leashes are considered a sort of 'holy grail' of leashes. Many puppy owners seek out good quality cotton leashes and a few find ones that function well for them. So, what's the appeal of a cotton leash? Well, quite simply they are soft and work well for puppies who enjoy getting themselves wet and/or if you live in an area prone to water and rain. They are durable but you ought to be careful because they can in some instances cause leash burn if your puppy like to pull the leash while he/she is wearing it.

Q. What leash should I buy if my puppy has health problems?

This is a common question and unambiguously, I would always advise that you speak to your vet. Sorry to reminisce on this but you need to speak to your vet about your puppy's personal requirements. This is important and it's even more important not to second guess the situation because you need to keep your puppy's personal and physical safety as an absolute priority. What I will say though, is that harnesses are great for all puppies, especially those with physical health issues. Extra support means you'll have a puppy who is less prone to injuries and further complications.

Housetraining

Q. When is the best time to housetrain my puppy?

The perfect time is between 12 and 16 weeks old, however if you bring your puppy home when he/she is older, house training will take longer than expected. However, keep with it and if he/she is struggling after this time, seek a reputable training centre.

Q. What timings should I keep to when house-training my puppy?

It's always advised that you take your puppy outside when you first wake up in the morning. The earlier the better. After this, every hour (although 45 mins will do - if you can manage it). Before bed, make sure to let your puppy eliminate at least once - you don't want to have to keep getting up throughout the night!

Q. Can I use a crate when house breaking my puppy?

Absolutely - and this is actually a great method to help the process along but crating for housetraining purposes should always be a short term solution and not a permanent one by any means.

The best way to housetrain with the use of crating is to ensure in the first instance that you have a large crate. It must be big enough for your puppy to lie down in and to comfortably turn his/her body around.

- -

I now want to address general questions that a person might have with concerns to all things puppy-related.

Q. Are there reasons why I shouldn't get a puppy?

Yes, there are many reasons why puppies are not suitable for some people. Besides the obvious reasons why a person might not get dogs in general (they aren't 'dog people'), you need to keep some things in mind before committing to getting a puppy. Here are the reasons why a person might not make the most ideal puppy owner.

1. If you can't commit.

Puppies are not like kittens or many other baby animals. They require constant care and need exercise, proper feeding, and proper training. This is taxing and you have to be prepared for this. Especially as they grow into adulthood when they'll be even more active, if you are by nature a lazy person or for whatever other reason you are not able to dedicate the physical and emotion energy it take to own and look after a puppy, it's best to give them a miss.

2. If you have a (**VERY**) busy life.

Equally, if you have a very full-on life-style due to long hours at work or other reasons, owning a puppy is doing them and yourself a disservice.

3. If you aren't willing to learn.

Your puppy has a lot to learn and so do you! Many first time puppy owners lean how to care for their little fluffy friends with dedication. If you aren't willing to take on the task, there is no reason for you to get a puppy.

4. Because you find them 'cute'.

Don't get me wrong - puppies are so adorable! But that's no reason to get a puppy on that basis alone.

Puppies are sentient and intelligent animals. You should be in it for the companionship and to give a beautiful animal a home - not just for the looks. The cuteness of a puppy is a perk but that's all it is - it should never be the reason you get one because when that thrill rubs off, will you want to keep your dog? If the answer is no, do your potential puppy a favour and let him/her go to a loving and deserving household.

To contrast, there are far more reasons why one **would** choose to adopt a puppy as opposed to not adopting one. Either way, it's important to make a rational and well reasoned decision based on being informed about what to expect when you get a puppy. With that said, let's look at reasons why puppies will benefit your life or in other words, why you should indeed get a puppy.

1. You will feel happier.

It's been known for a long time in anthrozoology and even interdisciplinary psychology that owning a puppy can help manage symptoms of depression - especially loneliness. Having a puppy around will give you a sense of purpose, oblige you to stay active (which increases endorphins in the brain leading to feeling happier overall), and make you feel less alone in this complicated and unpredictable world.

2. Puppies are loyal and *will* love you.

If you love and respect your puppy, they will love you - by showing you undying love and affection, their loyalty will cure any stress you hold at the end of a day, in an instant.

3. You'll become very popular everywhere you go.

People love a cute puppy they randomly come across in the street. I warn you though - you'll be bombarded by questions, attention and your puppy will be the recipient of many a cuddle from strangers. It's a beautiful moment that you can share with someone who has the same appreciation for dogs that you do. And even if they don't, you turned a few heads in the process.

4. Puppies can help you to regain a sense of innocence.

The world is a dark and unforgiving place - especially if you have a lot of stress to deal with. It can often feel like your innocence and beautiful naivety was taken away a long time ago. But when you have a puppy to come home to, all of that innocence returns in the form of an adorable fluffy face that is craving attention and some food. And as you look at your adorable little puppy, you realize that the world can't be all that bad with something *this* cute in it.

Conclusion

As we come to the end of this puppy training guide, I would like to say thank you for choosing this book. It is my hope that you found the information within these pages to be useful. Remember that while this guide is deigned to be an introductory course in managing all things puppy-related from day one, puppy training and care isn't a single event. It's something that you are responsible of from the day you bring your puppy home until the day that he/she grows into an adult dog. Your dog deserves to be treated as not only a friend and companion, but also a family member who is worthy of unconditional love and whose love is reciprocated if proper care and treatment is in place within a household. With all puppies and dogs in general, there is a major trust factor which, in every case, has to work both ways.

If you respect and love your puppy unfailingly, they're the most rewarding animals to own, whether you rescued them or bought them. Dogs can be one of the best elements of the human experience and ensuring they grow up happy and healthy begins with you looking after them and training them properly during the earliest stages of puppyhood. Puppy training isn't always straight forward and mistakes will be made. Every animal is an individual and not all sizes fit all when it comes to advice but the principles of this guide are a good outline to get you started.

All the best going forward, for both you and your puppy!

\- \-

Printed in Great Britain
by Amazon

50056830R00071